D0247984
MY DAY
AT THE
ZOO
BIRD
PARADISE
Terry Jennings
QED
QED Publishing

Consultant: Steve Parker
Editor: Eve Marleau
Designer and
Picture Researcher: Liz Wiffen

First published in the UK in 2010 by
QED Publishing
A Quarto Group Company
226 City Road
London EC1V 2TT

www.qed-publishing.co.uk

ISBN 978 1 84835 470 8

Printed in China

Picture credits
Key: t=top, b=bottom, r=right, l=left, c=centre
Getty 9b Leticia Lovo
Photolibrary 4b JTB Photo, 5t JTB Photo, 5b Wayne Lynch, 12b jspix jspix, 17b Mark Jones, 19b Mike Powles
Shutterstock 1t & folios Chen Wei Seng, 1b ksyproduktor, 2b pandapaw, 3r Volodymyr Krasyuk, 6t FloridaStock, 6b Reddogs, 7t H. Tuller, 8t JKlingebiel, 9t Eric Isselée, 10 Milena, 11r Eric Isselée, 11l Pichugin Dmitry, 12t pandapaw, 13t Jill Lang, 14t Luca Bertolli, 14b Brian Prawl, 15t Jaros, 16c Christian Musat, 17t M. Uptegrove, 18t John Carnemolla, 19t NSemprevivo, 20t Christian Wilkinson, 20b Reinhold Leitner, 21r Gentoo Multimedia Ltd., 22b Gentoo Multimedia Ltd.
stock.xchange all pages (foliage borders) TouTouke & straymuse, 6b 11l 12b 17t 19t 20b porah, 13b 14b 17b satty4u

The words in **bold** are explained in the Glossary on page 22.

Contents

Birds and bird parks 4
Eagles 6
Vultures 8
Parrots 10
Peacocks 12
Flamingos and storks 14
Pelicans 16
Ostriches 18
Penguins 20
Glossary 22
Index 23
Notes for parents and teachers 24

Birds and bird parks

Today we are going to a bird park. A bird park has lots of big cages called aviaries that the birds live in.

Bird watch

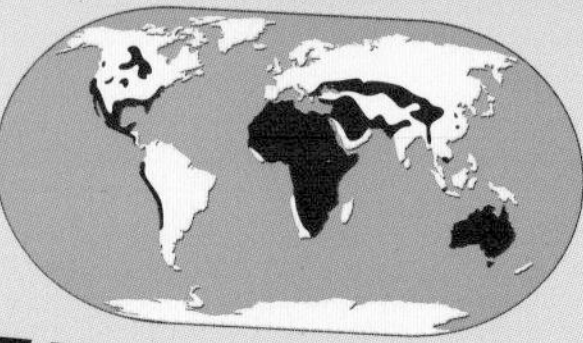

The map shows where in the world the animal is from. Information about the most rare or at risk animals is given when you see the **endangered** symbol.

The birds in a bird park come from all over the world. Birds are the only animals that have feathers. All birds have a mouth called a **beak**, two legs and two wings. Birds lay eggs with a shell, and most birds can fly.

→ Inside a large aviary at a bird park.

↑ Some birds in a bird park are able to walk around freely.

Some of the aviaries in bird parks are so big you can walk through them. Many of the birds that live near water are out in the open where you can see them easily, while a few kinds wander around among the people. It's a bird paradise!

→ Toucans have a very large beak.

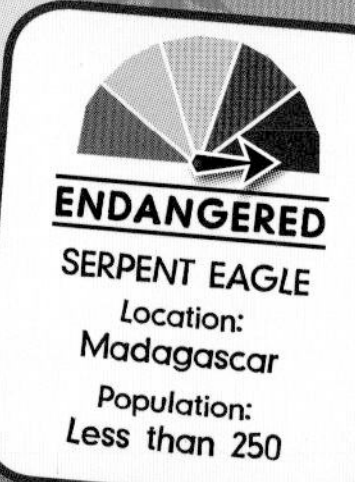

Eagles

Eagles are very large birds of prey. They live in mountains and forests all over the world.

American bald eagle

One of the biggest birds I saw was an American bald eagle. It had large feet with sharp claws, called **talons**. The bald eagle uses its feet to grab hold of prey and its beak to tear up food.

↑ The **wingspan** of an American bald eagle can be up to 2.4 metres.

→ The American bald eagle has white feathers on its head and neck.

Another aviary I visited had a golden eagle in it. This eagle had a dark-brown back and pale head and neck. Golden eagles live in places where there are few people around, such as on mountains or over cliffs by the sea.

→ **Like all eagles, the golden eagle has very good eyesight.**

ZOO VIEW

The white-tailed sea eagle is the fourth largest eagle in the world. It became **extinct** in Britain in 1918. In 1975, a few sea eagles were brought to an island off the coast of Scotland. They had babies, and now there are more than 200 sea eagles in Scotland.

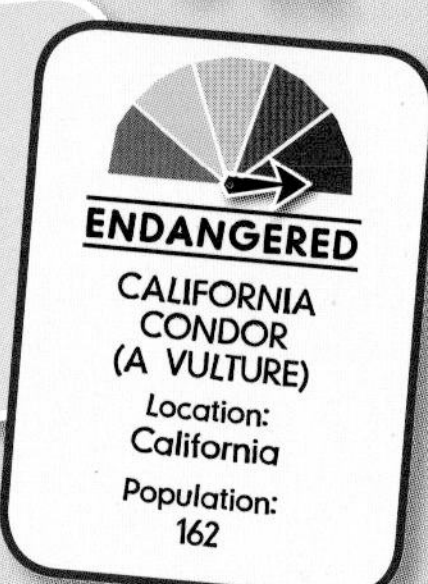

Vultures

Vultures are large birds. Unlike other birds, they have no feathers on their head or neck. Vultures are found in many countries all over the world.

↓ A vulture has a bald head and neck to stop its feathers from getting dirty when feeding.

Vultures feed on rotting meat left by eagles, lions and other animals. Having no feathers on their head helps to keep them clean. They have very good eyesight and can spot food from a long way away.

An organization called Vulture Rescue is trying to increase the numbers of vultures. They are trying to **breed** them in captivity, so that they can be released into the wild later.

At the bird park, I learned that vultures do an important job because they clean up bodies left by hunting animals. These bodies would otherwise attract flies and germs.

↑ Vultures use their large wings to fly around for hours, looking for dead animals.

→ These vultures feeding at a rubbish dump are not fussy about what they eat.

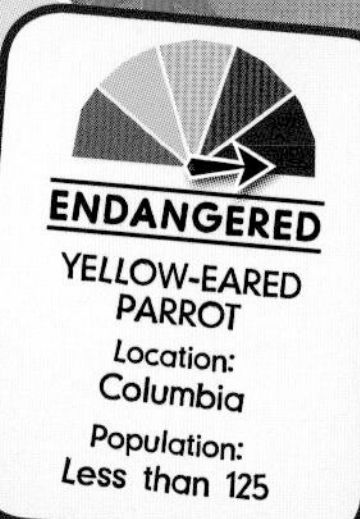

Parrots

Parrots come from the warmer countries of the world, such as Australia.

Most parrots are brightly coloured. The parrot I saw was a green-winged macaw from South America. It lives at the top of tall trees.

↑ The green-winged macaw feeds on fruits, seeds and nuts.

Three things you didn't know about... PARROTS

1. There are 353 different species of parrot in the world.
2. Parrots can live for up to 80 years in the wild.
3. Many parrots can imitate, or copy, human voices.

There are many different species of parrot. Cockatoos are found in Australia. Lovebirds are small parrots from Africa and Madagascar. They get their name from the way they sit together in pairs, resting their heads against each other.

↓ **African lovebirds like these ones are always found in pairs.**

↓ **In Australia, sulphur-crested cockatoos live in large flocks.**

Peacocks

The peacocks at the bird park were walking around in the open, following the visitors.

Peacocks first came from Asia, but they have lived in parks and large gardens in Europe for thousands of years.

tail feathers

↑ The peacock has the longest tail feathers of any bird.

peahen

→ The peahen is a dull brown colour. This makes her hard to see when sitting on her eggs.

babies

↑ The peacock can spread his tail out like a fan to attract a mate.

The male peacock has the longest tail feather of any kind of bird. The female (called a peahen) is a dull brown colour. Although peacocks and peahens feed on the ground, they sleep high in trees at night, safe from most enemies.

ZOO STARS

Percy the peacock lives in a village in Lincolnshire, England. When Percy found a mate, he became a nuisance with his loud screeches. Now people in the village are arguing about whether he should stay!

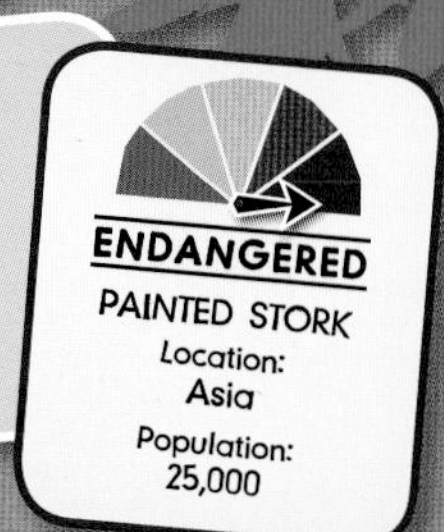

Flamingos and storks

Flamingos live in large groups on shallow lakes in Africa, South America, Asia and southern Europe. Flamingos are a kind of wading bird.

Flamingos feed on shrimps and other water animals. They catch these by wading through water, moving their beak from side to side to sieve food from the water.

↑ Flamingos sieve tiny animals from the water with their specially shaped beak.

→ Flamingos stand on one leg for many hours at a time, even when they are asleep.

Storks are also wading birds. They spend the winter in Africa and in summer **migrate** to Europe to build their nests. At the bird park, I saw two storks sitting on a huge nest on a wooden platform in a tree. In some parts of Europe, storks nest on the chimneys of houses.

ZOO STARS

Two scientists in America studied flamingos to find out why they often stand on one leg. Eventually, the scientists found the answer – standing on one leg stops the flamingo's body losing too much heat. They swap legs to stop each leg becoming too cold.

↑ In some parts of Europe, white storks nest on house chimneys. Some people believe it is lucky to have storks nesting on your house.

Pelicans

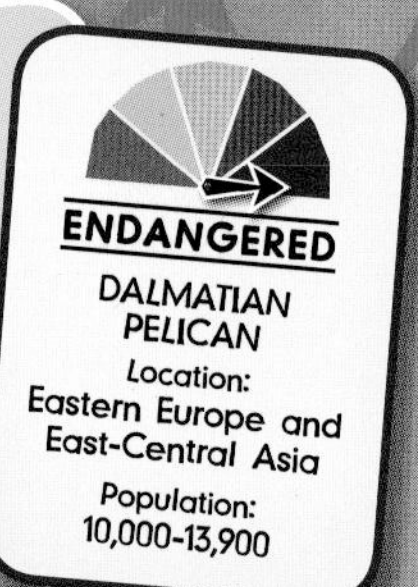

At the bird park, I saw some pelicans. They are large seabirds.

The pelican's *beak* has a huge **pouch** that holds three times as much as its stomach. It uses the pouch to scoop up fish from the water and also to collect water to drink. Fully stretched, the pouch can hold as much as a large *bucket*.

pouch

← The pelican's pouch lets it eat a lot of food quickly.

The brown pelican of North and South America catches fish by diving into the sea. American white pelicans work together to catch fish. They form a line and herd fish in front of them into the shallow water. There the fish are easy to catch.

↑ The pelican dives down to scoop up fish in the water.

↑ Baby pelicans take food from their mother's and father's beaks.

ZOO STARS

In 1976, a pelican called Mr Percival from Adelaide Zoo, Australia, was the star of a film called 'Storm Boy', which was about a boy who looks after pelicans.

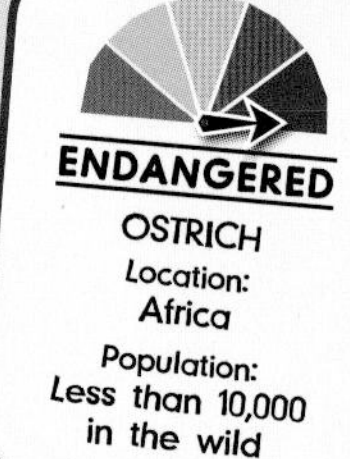

Ostriches

Not all birds can fly. Although they have small wings, the world's biggest birds – ostriches – cannot fly.

→ Although an ostrich cannot fly, it can run very fast from danger.

Three things you didn't know about... OSTRICHES

1. Most birds have four toes, but an ostrich has only two.
2. An ostrich has the largest eye of any land animal. It measures 5 centimetres across.
3. An ostrich's egg weighs about 1.7 kilograms.

Ostriches run at speeds of up to 70 kilometres an hour, which helps them to escape enemies such as lions. Ostriches live on the dry grasslands of Africa.

Female ostriches lay their eggs in a nest on the ground. The eggs are the biggest of all birds. The male ostrich sits on the eggs to keep them warm at night. The female sits on the eggs during the day.

↑ The eggs of an ostrich are the largest of any bird.

← Male ostriches are black and white. They can grow to be 2.8 metres tall. The females are smaller and greyish-brown.

Penguins

Penguins live near some of the world's coldest seas. Penguins cannot fly, but they can swim better than any other bird.

Penguins swim using their small, stiff wings like paddles. They use their tail and feet for steering. While they are swimming, penguins hunt for fish and shrimps to eat.

← These Adelie penguins live among the ice and snow of Antarctica.

Adelie penguins

→ Penguins use their small, stiff wings to swim underwater in search of fish and shrimps.

The emperor penguin is the largest of all penguins. It can grow to 120 centimetres tall and weigh up to 37 kilograms.

In the winter, the female emperor penguin lays one egg. She then goes out to sea and doesn't return until spring. The male balances the egg on his feet to keep it warm. When the baby hatches, it stays close to its father for the first few weeks.

← 120 centimetres tall

Emperor penguin

↑ The emperor penguin does not build a nest. Instead, the male keeps his chick warm under a flap of skin on his stomach.

Three things you didn't know about... PENGUINS

1. There are at least 18 different kinds of penguin.
2. A penguin can hold its breath for about 20 minutes under water.
3. Penguins use a kind of sign language to 'talk' to each other.

Glossary

Aviary A place to keep birds in.

Beak The hard part of a bird's mouth.

Breed To produce babies.

Endangered Describes an animal or plant that is in danger of becoming extinct.

Extinct Not existing anymore; when every one of a kind of animal or plant has died out.

Migrate To go to another country, or another part of the country, where more food can be found.

Pouch A bag for carrying things.

Prey An animal that is hunted by other animals for food.

Talon One of the large claws on the foot of an eagle, owl or some other bird of prey.

Wading Walking through water.

Wingspan The distance from one end of a bird's wing to the end of its other wing.

Index

Adelie penguin 20
African lovebird 11
American bald eagle 6
American white pelican 17
aviary 4, 5, 22

beak 4, 5, 14, 16, 22
birds of prey 6, 22
brown pelican 17

California condor 8
cockatoos 11

Dalmatian pelican 16

eagles 6–7, 22
eggs 4, 18, 19, 21
emperor penguin 21

feathers 4, 5, 6, 12, 13
flamingos 14–15

golden eagle 7
green peafowl 12
green-winged macaw 10

Humboldt penguin 20

lovebirds 11

ostriches 18–19

painted stork 14
parrots 10–11
peacocks 12–13
pelicans 16–17
penguins 20–21

seabirds 16
serpent eagle 6
storks 15
sulphur-crested cockatoo 11

tails 5, 12, 13, 20
talons 6, 22
toucans 5

vultures 8–9

wading birds 14, 15
white stork 15
white-tailed sea eagle 7
wings 4, 5, 9, 18, 20, 22

yellow-eared parrot 10

Notes for parents and teachers

- Discuss with children why it is necessary to be quiet and not run when visiting a bird park. Why is it necessary for them to wash their hands carefully after touching a bird or any part of its aviary, and particularly before touching food?
- In the world as a whole, there are about 9000 species of wild bird. How many kinds of birds do children know? You can, if you wish, point out that most birds lay their eggs in a nest. In some species, when the young birds hatch they are blind and naked. In other species, particularly those birds that nest on the ground, the young are able to run around soon after they hatch. Can children think of examples of both kinds of birds?
- Discuss with children what is meant by extinction and why some birds are in danger of becoming extinct. The main causes of extinction are hunting, the effects of pollution and the destruction of the birds' natural habitat. If bird parks and zoos are able to breed endangered birds, they will not be able to release them into the wild unless a suitable safe place can be found for them.
- What birds visit the area around your home? Keep a bird diary. If you have a garden, feed the birds regularly and also provide them with clean water for drinking and bathing. A simple bird table or bird feeder is quite easy for a child to make with adult help. If you have suitable trees or walls, erect bird nestboxes. All of these devices provide excellent ways for children to study common birds closely.
- Some useful websites for more information:

  www.allaboutbirds.org

  www.bbc.co.uk/nature/animals/birds

  www.rspb.org.uk

  www.kids.yahoo.com/animals/birds

  www.kidwings.com/index.htm

  www.nwf.org/wildlife

  www.thebigzoo.com

  www.arkive.org

  www.uksafari.com

  www.defenders.org/wildlife__and__habitat